THE POCKET Houseplants

Published in 2026
by Gemini Gift Books
Part of Gemini Books Group

Based in Woodbridge and London

Marine House, Tide Mill Way,
Woodbridge, Suffolk IP12 1AP
United Kingdom

www.geminibooks.com

Part of the Gemini Pockets series

Text by Becky Freeth
Cover image: Shutterstock/deckorator

ISBN 978-1-80247-314-8

A CIP catalogue record for this book is available from the British Library.

Manufacturer's EU Representative: Eurolink Compliance Limited, 25 Herbert Place, Dublin, D02 AY86, Republic of Ireland. admin@eurolink-europe.ie

Printed in China

10 9 8 7 6 5 4 3 2 1

MIX
Paper | Supporting responsible forestry
FSC® C117745

Picture Credits: 4, 7, 10, 18, 42, 56, 57, 62, 63, 70, 71, 72, 73, 96, 97, 114, 115, 122, 123: Shutterstock/Jeanna Draw; 8, 11, [illegible], [illegible], [illegible], [illegible], [illegible], [illegible], [illegible], 112, 113, 116, 118, 119: Shutterstock/ Prokhorovich; 15, 36, 44, 88, 89, 90, 110, 111: Freepik; 16, 17, 26, 27, 35, 37, 39, 41: Adobe Stock; 24, 25, 30, 31, 50, 51, 58, 59, 60, 61, 64, 65, 66, 68, 69, 80, 81, 82, 83, 98, 99, 106, 107, 120, 121, 126, 127: Shutterstock/GooseFrol; 52, 53, 54: Shutterstock/roughedges_stock; 74, 75: Shutterstock/ GoodStudio; 76, 77, 78: Shutterstock/ kaiwut niponkaew; 84, 85: Shutterstock/N.Petrosyan; 86, 87: Shutterstock/ Affan_Mochammad; 100, 101: Shutterstock/aba_inside; 102, 103, 104: Shutterstock/Julia Lullula; 108, 109: Shutterstock/ Natalia Babakhina; 124/125: Shutterstock/maljuk

THE POCKET

Houseplants

G:

CONTENTS

Introduction

Some of us are born with green fingers, others have to learn. Either way, there's no such thing as "pot luck" when it comes to keeping houseplants, they need to be properly looked after.

As with people and pets, indoor plants need food, the right environment and plenty of care and attention. From there, they rely on varying levels of sunlight, warmth and water depending on their species, so finding the right one to cohabit with – or keeping them happy when you do – is not always as straightforward as it seems.

That said, the more humans learn about plants, the more we realize that we need them as much as they need us. It's been scientifically proven that certain types of greenery purify our air, increase our productivity and lower our stress levels; others can noticeably improve our moods.

A happy home is one filled with houseplants – and this handy guide will help you to become the perfect plant parent for your leafy housemates.

INTRODUCTION

Chapter One

The Basics

A brief history of houseplants

Welcoming the outdoors in might seem like a fresh idea – especially now we know the benefits of plants for our mental and physical health. But around 5,000 years ago, the ancient Egyptians were some of the first people to welcome plants like ferns and palm trees into the home as decoration.

Collecting household plants became popular in Europe during the Victorian era and spread to the US and Australia after World War II as more and more species suitable for growing indoors became available.

By the 1960s, houseplants were highly fashionable, and no home was complete without a thriving collection. Snake plants, begonias and Devil's ivy were among the favourites, but the real star was the exotic and highly sought-after Swiss cheese plant, which was printed all over linens and upholstery as well as taking pride of place in sitting rooms across the land.

Ever since the global pandemic, interest in the mood-boosting companionship of houseplants has been growing, and, suddenly, everyone wants to know their "Flamingo flower" from their "Fiddle-leaf fig".

Health Benefits of House Plants

BOOST YOUR MOOD: Humans have an inherent desire to connect with nature

CALMING: Green is a soothing colour to have around the home

REDUCE STRESS: Some plants have been shown to lower blood pressure

CLEAR THE AIR: They have been found to reduce harmful pollutants in our air

IMPROVE FOCUS: Oxygenating plants can promote thinking

INCREASE SLEEP: Scented plants like lavender and jasmine boost relaxation

HEAL: Aloe vera plants have medicinal properties for burns and wounds

RELEASE TENSION: Peace lilies ease headaches by absorbing air toxins

“We can live without every other science, but we cannot live without plants. They are our food, our lungs, our strengths, our relaxation, our pleasure, our future and our hope.”

Andi Mellis, Botanist

Getting Started

Step One: Choose

It's easy to pick a plant on appearances, but if it doesn't suit your home or lifestyle, this beautiful relationship won't last long. Weigh up all the unique advantages of certain species (such as air purification) and the downsides (such as maintenance) with equal importance

Step Two: Buy

Reputable retailers like garden centres or nurseries will keep your plant in good condition right up to the point of sale. Supermarkets or shops that don't specialize in plant care may sell plants showing signs of over- or underwatering or have browning or yellow leaves.

Timing matters, too. Avoid buying houseplants in the cold of winter, when sudden changes in temperature are likely to shock the leaves.

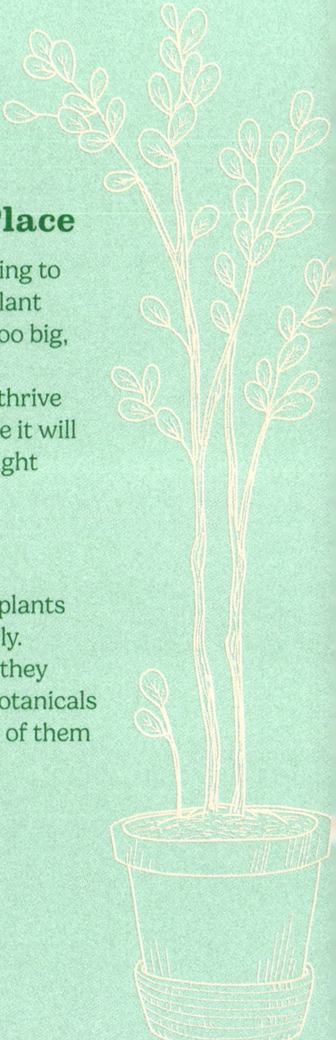

Step Three: Pot & Place

A pot doesn't have to add anything to the aesthetic of your amazing plant but it must be practical: never too big, too small or lacking drainage. Consider where your plant will thrive in your home, rather than where it will look best. Think: temperature, light and humidity.

Step Four: Love

Once they settle in, most houseplants quickly become part of the family. Nearly half of plant owners say they feel "deeply connected" to the botanicals they welcome in, often thinking of them more like friends or children.

Choosing a Plant

Three things to consider

Is it safe around animals?

Remember, any plant sitting at low level is within reach of pets or children, so beware of species that are toxic when ingested.

Do you have enough room?

Firstly, do you have enough space for a plant that grows rapidly, either vertically or horizontally? Secondly, do you have enough variation in light and temperature to move a plant if it's not happy?

Can you give it everything it needs?

Some plants need more commitment than others. If this is your first foray into plant ownership — or you've been unlucky in the past — look for an easy-care companion that's practically unkillable.

Most Popular Houseplants Around the World*

North America
Swiss cheese plant (*Monstera deliciosa*)

South America
Blue passionflower (*Passiflora caerulea*)

Europe
Swiss cheese plant

Middle East & Central Asia
Rose bay (*Nerium oleander*)

Asia and Oceania
Swiss cheese plant

Africa
Yellow sage (*Lantana camara*)

** Based on Google search data, 2022*

Cleaner AND Greener

NASA scientists have identified certain plants that leave your environment better than they found it. Not only do they release oxygen, but they also absorb carbon dioxide and remove nasty pollutants like benzene, formaldehyde and trichloroethylene.

These are the easiest air-cleansing plants to source and live with:

1. Chinese evergreen
2. Devil's ivy
3. Peace lily
4. Spider palm
5. Snake plant

Houseplants can increase productivity in the workplace by as much as 38 per cent. One study at an English university showed that students worked harder and more creatively in an environment with houseplants. Even levels of happiness were significantly improved among the group.

University of Exeter study (2013)

Gifting: The Best Plant Presents and What They Symbolize

Poinsettia: Hope, peace and success

Orchid: Love, luxury and beauty

Jade plant: Happiness, wealth and prosperity

ZZ plant: Positive energy and protection

Peace lily: Hope, comfort and sympathy

Prayer plant: Gratitude

Chinese money plant: Good luck and fortune

Calathea: New beginnings

“He that plants trees loves others besides himself.”

Thomas Fuller, *Gnomologia: Adagies and Proverbs* (1732)

Basic Buying Guide

Golden rules for purchasing houseplants

- Thoroughly inspect the condition of the leaves, flowers and soil to guarantee the best start in your home.
- If conditions outside are cold, wrap up your new plant for the journey home to avoid temperature shock.
- Look up your plant's needs and start following them carefully as soon as they arrive in their new environment.
- Use the right soil. If you need to repot your plant, make sure they don't need a specialist mix before they bed in.

“Botany I rank with the most valuable sciences.”

Thomas Jefferson (1743-1826)

Potting ...

Elevated plant pots create a layered decorative feature that works well with trailing plants growing elegantly over the edges.

Hanging planters create height in your display, but they are also practical when you lack shelf space or a window ledge to catch the sun.

Terrariums are small glass containers that regulate heat and humidity conditions, like a green house. A sealed terrarium is a happy place for ferns, while an open terrarium is great for sun lovers, like cacti.

Decorative pots are an ideal way to frame a beloved botanical. If your pot doesn't have holes in the bottom, repot it inside a plastic planter with drainage, then hide that inside the ornamental one.

… and Where to Place

Plants by room

Bathroom

Boston fern, Calathea, Nerve plant and Air plants thrive in moisture-rich shower rooms where, in return, they can protect the space against condensation.

Living space

Choose air-purifying plants, such as the Peace lily, to create a soothing space, especially if they are non-toxic, like the Parlour or Areca palms, which will cohabit safely with pets or children.

Kitchen

Hardy plants that can withstand fluctuations in temperature and enjoy humidity, such as the Dragon tree or Spider plant, are happy in cooking spaces.

Bedroom

To promote sleep and feelings of calm, go for an air-purifying plant that improves oxygen levels, like a Peace lily or Calathea.

Hallway

The pleasantly scented White jasmine is an ideal option for an entry way to give guests a warm welcome. Just make sure the space has enough good light.

Home office

If you're looking for an aesthetically pleasing office plant that helps boost productivity, just make sure it can withstand the conditions. The laid-back Radiator plant could make a good desk mate because it quite likes heaters.

"Gardens are not made by singing 'Oh, how beautiful, and sitting in the shade.'"

'The Glory of the Garden',
Rudyard Kipling, 1911

Grow Your Own Way

It may sound like an old wives' tale but playing music to your plants really can help your indoor garden grow.

Studies show that houseplants react positively to the subtle vibrations of classical or jazz music, which can increase growth. Higher volumes and stronger vibrations seem to have the opposite effect.

Even talking to them at low level on a regular basis can apparently improve photosynthesis and a plant's ability to fight infection, so bonding with your green guests really is worth your energy.

Soil Mates

Your first plant is rarely ever your last, and once you fall in love with indoor gardening, maintaining your plant menagerie takes on a new lease of life.

For instance, if you didn't know that plants could talk to each other, it's worth thinking about who they sit next to.

It's true, plants can effectively tell each other to "back off" by releasing chemicals called volatile organic compounds (VOCs). In fact, science shows growth can be negatively affected when we put plants so close they can touch.

Compatible Plants

Compatible plants are those that appreciate the same living conditions. After that, they can be arranged by texture, colour or height.

These botanical besties grow well together:

Peace lily & Devil's ivy: One grows up and the other grows down, but both like indirect light and moist soil.

Snake plant & ZZ plant: These two are happy in low light with very little access to water.

Cacti & String of pearls: Strikingly different shapes and textures make an interesting desertscape.

Dragon tree & Fiddle-leaf fig: When grouping large and small, put the tallest at the back to allow equal access to light.

Chapter Two

Problem Solving

No Such Thing as Pot Luck

Don't be disheartened if your plant starts to look unhappy in your home. From spots on the leaves to yellow and brown tinges, or wilting and drop-off, all plants have a way of hinting at the problem. With a quick and informed response, there's every chance an unhealthy plant can be saved.

Symptom: Heavy Leaf Fall

- ☐ **Shock**
  Your plant could be reacting to a sudden change in temperature, light or moisture levels after being moved or repotted.

Solution: Allow a healthy plant a few days to readjust.

- ☐ **Over- or underwatering**
  Check the compost – is it dried out or too moist? Your plant may need more or less than you think.

Solution: Water a thirsty plant or pour away excess water collected at the bottom.

- ☐ **Pest damage**
  Inspect the soil for signs of infestation.

Solution: Look for suitable pesticides.

Symptom: Yellow Leaves

- ☐ **Hungry**
  Research your plant's fertilizer needs, it could be lacking essential nutrients.

Solution: Feed according to their care instructions, but don't overfeed!

- ☐ **Over or underwatering**
  Compost that is too compact and dry or too wet will upset certain plants.

Solution: Leave the plant to dry out or give it a much-needed drink.

- ☐ **Too cold**
  Is your plant sitting in a draught? Flowering plants like African violet and Poinsettia hate a cold breeze.

Solution: Try a new location.

Symptom: Brown Leaf Tips

- ☐ **Dry air**
  Plants like the Boston fern, Calathea and Jasmine love moisture in the air because of the humid countries they're native to.

Solution: Mist the leaves regularly or move the pot to a bathroom.

- ☐ **Over or underwatering**
  Brown leaves from excess watering or extreme thirst won't heal, but proper care should help the plant grow more leaflets.

Solution: Adjust your watering habits, especially as the seasons change.

- ☐ **Too much sun**
  Shade-loving plants will go brown in too much direct sun.

Solution: Move them out of bright light.

Symptom: Curling Leaves

☐ **Too hot**
In warmer homes, compost could be drying out too fast to quench your plant's thirst. Heaters in winter and hot, direct sunlight in summer are common causes.

Solution: Move them to a cooler spot.

☐ **Underwatering**
When they've been starved of water, some plants curl their leaves away from the sun to limit evaporation.

Solution: Water plentifully, enough to run through drainage holes at the bottom.

☐ **Pest damage**
Thoroughly check the leaves and soil for signs of disease.

Solution: Identify and act on the problem with a pesticide.

Symptom: Holey Leaves

☐ **Damage**
Pets and boisterous children in high-traffic areas can cause wear and tear to leaves.

Solution: Prune leaves regularly and move to a better-protected space.

☐ **Fungal disease**
Inspect the soil closely for signs of fungal infection. By the time it has affected the leaves, this could already be advanced.

Solution: Move to a well-ventilated space and give them time to adjust to it before looking for a treatment.

☐ **Pest problem**
Look out for signs that your plant's leaves are being nibbled by a pest.

Solution: Identify the pest and act fast.

Symptom: Spotty Leaves

- ☐ **Overwatering**
  If you see dark brown spots emerge, check the compost is not too saturated - a sign that it has more water than it needs.

Solution: Check the pot has drainage holes and leave to dry out on a draining board.

- ☐ **Underwatering**
  Dry patches are a sign that the plant is starved of water. Check the compost to see if your plant is thirsty.

Solution: Give it a good watering and keep the soil moist.

- ☐ **Hard water**
  Some plants react badly to the chemicals in hard tap water.

Solution: Switch to distilled/filtered water.

Symptom: Wilting Leaves

☐ **Root bound**
A pot that doesn't give a plant enough room for the roots to absorb water will stifle it.

Solution: Repot in a larger container.

☐ **Too hot**
Your plant could be sweltering in too much direct sun or artificial warmth.

Solution: Try placing them in a cooler location.

☐ **Over- or underwatering**
Depending on the type of plant, leaves will wilt from being either overwatered or underwatered.

Solution: Check the soil and change your watering habits.

Symptom: No Flowers

☐ **Too dark**
Most plants need sunlight for photosynthesis, even if indirect or dappled light is the best you can do indoors.

Solution: Move your plant to a sunnier spot.

☐ **Dry air**
A plant that's used to humid habitats won't flower when your home environment is starved of moisture.

Solution: Move to a kitchen or bathroom.

☐ **Too much room**
Not all plants love spacious pots. Some thrive when the roots are restricted within smaller pots.

Solution: Repot in a smaller plant pot.

Symptom: Flower Buds Fall

- [ ] **Dry air**
  Flowering in a dry environment is harder for plants that love a little humidity.

Solution: Mist the leaves or set on a tray of damp pebbles to increase moisture.

- [ ] **Too hot or cold**
  Extreme changes in temperature can put stress on the plant and cause flower buds to drop off suddenly.

Solution: Move away from air conditioning units or heaters.

- [ ] **Over- or underwatering**
  Check the soil for signs that your plant has had more or less water than they need.

Solution: Revisit your plant's specific needs and adjust your habits accordingly.

Busted: Five Myths About Plant Care

- **Keep to a watering schedule**
  Research and remember your plant's specific water needs but adapt them as you go to suit your environment.
- **Filtered water is best for houseplants**
  Distilled water lacks certain minerals that plants need to grow. Before using, allow tap water to sit overnight to dissipate harmful chemicals.
- **Succulents can survive without water**
  They may be used to arid environments, but succulents like Cacti still need a good watering, especially during summer.
- **All bugs are the enemy**
  It's true that some insects can do harm, but others are there to balance the ecosystem. Do your research before you intervene.
- **The bigger the pot, the better the growth**
  Give your plants enough space, but if you sit a small plant in too much soil it could easily become overwatered.

Make Your Own Potassium Feed

Banana peels soaked in water make a simple homemade fertilizer that can boost plant growth and flowering.

1. Cut leftover banana peels into small pieces around 1 inch (2-3 cm) in length.

2. Submerge in a bowl of clean water for 2-3 days.

3. When the peel is soft enough, strain the water into a pouring jug.

4. Feed your plants around the base with the strained liquid.

Best for: Orchids, Air plants, Swiss cheese plant and Devil's ivy.

Chapter Three

A TO Z OF HOUSEPLANTS

African Violet

Streptocarpus

SUN: Bright, indirect light

WATER: Soak in water for around 20 minutes when the soil gets dry

FERTILIZER: Look for a water-soluble high-phosphate feed

MAINTENANCE: Low

If you're looking for a pop of colour, the delightful African violet is an attractive and low-maintenance plant that can flower all year long. That's just two of the qualities that make this one of the most popular flowering plants for the home.

As the name suggests, the blooms emerge in clusters of purple, but an African violet is also available in blue, pink, red and white.

From summer to winter, you might find need to move the pot around the home in search of adequate light – just be sure to keep them out of a draught as they don't like a chill.

Air Plants

Tillandsia

SUN: Bright, indirect light – direct sun can scorch their leaves

WATER: Soak in water every 2–3 weeks

FERTILIZER: Feed with a ready made low-nitrogen fertilizer once a month

MAINTENANCE: Low

Here's a novel idea: an indoor plant that doesn't need a pot, soil or a place on the windowsill.

Air plants will literally grow on anything – from wall-mounted wire frames to hanging glass ornaments – thriving instead on air or moisture from the environment.

Notoriously easy to care for, this futuristic-looking plant is often suited to modern decor, particularly studio apartments or office environments where space to suit pickier plants is limited.

Aloe Vera

Aloe barbadensis miller

SUN: Bright, indirect light – best to keep on windowsills in full sun

WATER: Infrequently, only when the soil is dry

FERTILIZER: Feed with a balanced, water-soluble fertilizer diluted to half strength once every 2–3 months

MAINTENANCE: Low

Warning: *Toxic to animals and children if ingested*

Aside from being interesting to look at with its fleshy tentacles and spikes, the evergreen Aloe vera plant is handy to keep around for healing minor cuts and scrapes.

The succulent originally comes from the desert, so overwatering is a common downfall for Aloe owners who struggle to strike that complex balance.

It is otherwise notoriously easy to keep, and thrives in the room temperature of most homes. Watch it carefully because it has effective ways of telling you what it needs: if the leaves are yellow, it's thirsty; if they are limp and heavy, it's had too much water.

Aloe, Aloe, Aloe

The most-Googled houseplant on the planet* is not only a staple in every plant-friendly home, it is known as nature's healer and found as an ingredient in everything from skincare to digestive medicine. When cut open, the leaves release a clear gel which is effective for healing burns and cuts by coating wounds and stimulating the immune system to speed up healing.

** Based on data between 2017–2020*

"I believe the 21st century will confirm Aloe vera to be the greatest medicine mankind has ever known."

Lee Ritter, Doctor of Naturopathy

Areca Palm

Dypsis lutenscens

SUN: Bright, indirect light

WATER: Keep soil moist at all times

FERTILIZER: Feed with a balanced fertilizer every couple of months

MAINTENANCE: Low

Once an Areca palm settles in, it can grow comfortably with your family for up to 10 years.

Finding the right spot, in the light of a south-facing window and out of the chill of an air-conditioner, is the key to keeping them happy, so avoid dark, temperature-controlled offices, especially in summer.

Instead, freshen up a stale living room with an Areca palm because of its many benefits for humans. Not only does it create a mood-boosting atmosphere with its vibrant green leaves, it is known to be one of the most air-purifying plants available.

Boston Fern

Nephrolepis exaltata

SUN: Bright, indirect light

WATER: Mist leaves regularly and keep compost moist at all times

FERTILIZER: Apply half-strength, balanced liquid fertilizer from spring to autumn

MAINTENANCE: Low

Popular for its long, lacy leaves, the Boston fern is the queen of the indoor jungle.

It's often used to elevate dull spaces because of the way it explodes out of a decorative hanging basket, adding greenery at different heights to the obvious eye-level window ledge.

A steamy bathroom or high-humidity kitchen are the perfect places to keep it, and, by absorbing the moisture for itself, a Boston fern will help to reduce condensation and damp in moisture-prone rooms.

Cacti

Cactaceae

SUN: Mostly full sun

WATER: Little to none

FERTILIZER: None

MAINTENANCE: Low

From the flowering Orchid cactus and Devil's tongue to the distinctively-shaped Bunny ears and Old man varieties, just one cactus is never enough.

Needing low levels of water or fertilizer and just a low-frills place in the sun, the humble cacti is one of the easiest indoor plants to keep, and therefore the introduction of one can quickly turn into a collection.

Not everyone considers these succulents to be houseplants because they're so different from other types of greenery, but to most plant parents, that's all part of their charm.

Calathea

Calathea orbifolia

SUN: Moderate, indirect light

WATER: Water little and often, and keep in a humid environment

FERTILIZER: Feed with a weak dose of nitrogen-rich fertilizer once a month during growing season

MAINTENANCE: Medium

Though popular, Calathea are demanding house plants best-suited to more advanced owners.

For starters, they need consistent warmth and humidity – no sudden fluctuations in temperature – and enjoy lots of light, although not too much. Find them a steamy spot, like a shower room, but don't overwater the soil.

If you can strike this balance, the reward is a lush, leafy plant companion who will comfortably cohabit with a fern (page 58) in the more humid corners of your home.

Chinese Evergreen

Aglaonema commutatum

SUN: Low-moderate, indirect light

WATER: Water thoroughly when the soil is dry to the touch – always allow the water to drain from the bottom of the pot

FERTILIZER: From spring to summer, feed with a balanced liquid fertilizer

MAINTENANCE: Low

Warning: *Toxic to animals and children if ingested*

Ideal for beginners, the Chinese evergreen is a tolerant plant that offers maximum results with minimal effort.

Unlike most indoor plants, this one doesn't expect many special conditions. It can live happily in low-level light, with little water, around dry air and promises to stick around for quite some time breathing fresh life into formerly dark spaces.

The Chinese evergreen does occasionally grow flowers that look like Peace lilies, but these are best cut back so that the plant can preserve its energy for growing vibrant, healthy foliage.

Symbolism: Luck, Abundance, Endurance, Strength, Energy

The Chinese evergreen is a symbol of good luck in Eastern Asia. It represents strength and resilience because it lives for a long time and renews its leaves whenever it loses them. In Feng Shui, this plant is a water element, believed to balance the energies of your space, thereby improving the sense of calm and reducing stress.

“Plant seeds of happiness, hope, success, and love; it will all come back to you in abundance. This is the law of nature.”

Steve Maraboli, *Life, the Truth, and Being Free* (2012)

Chinese Money Plant

Pilea peperomioides

SUN: Bright, indirect light

WATER: Water only when the soil is dry

FERTILIZER: Feed with a balanced, diluted liquid fertilizer once a month

MAINTENANCE: Low

It's true: money doesn't grow on trees. But, one of the reasons *Pilea* got the name "Chinese money plant" is because its round leaves overlap like a healthy stack of coins.

Ironically, the Chinese money plant can be quite expensive and hard to find, though it is easy to propagate from other plants and has affectionately become known as a "friendship" or "pass it along" plant. Fast-growing baby stems regularly grow at the base of the plant which can be simply removed and repotted as a gift for a fellow plant-lover.

Devil's Ivy

Epipremnum Aureum

SUN: Can survive in shade but prefers bright, indirect light

WATER: Water every 1–2 weeks in summer and once a month in winter

FERTILIZER: From spring to autumn, feed with a balanced liquid fertilizer

MAINTENANCE: Low

Warning: *Toxic to animals and children if ingested*

Even the most forgetful plant owner can generally maintain a Devil's ivy — and perhaps that's the key to its popularity.

Aside from it being virtually indestructible, one of the most attractive things about a Devil's ivy (sometimes called Golden pothos) is its elegant, trailing stems that make an interesting focal point in any room.

Set them on a tall plant stand or add them to a hanging basket; let them climb down from a high bookshelf or burst out of a vertical garden. However you decide to decorate with Devil's ivy, your faithful plant is a guaranteed talking point.

Dragon Tree

Dracaena marginata

SUN: Can tolerate shade but prefers bright, indirect light

WATER: Every three weeks

FERTILIZER: Feed lightly at the beginning of growing season with a balanced liquid fertilizer

MAINTENANCE: Low

Warning: *Toxic to animals and children if ingested*

If you're looking for an indoor tree, the Dragon tree is an easy entry-level option. They need very little care or attention – to the point where it's hard to go too far wrong.

Visually, the exotic Dragon tree is a stunning addition to the home. It has long, thin leaves that are sometimes lined in fiery, dragon red.

Treat them right and they could be a housemate for up to 15 years, peacefully purifying the air in your home by removing contaminants such as benzene, xylene and toluene.

False Shamrock

Oxalis triangularis

SUN: Bright, indirect light

WATER: Once a week, allowing the water to drain from the bottom of the pot

FERTILIZER: Feed with a high-potassium liquid fertilizer every 3–4 weeks

MAINTENANCE: Low

Warning: *Toxic to animals and children if ingested*

Living with a False shamrock is unlike many houseplant companions because it follows the rhythms of day and night, like humans or pets.

The deep purple plant will effectively "sleep when you sleep", curling up its three triangular leaflets as the daylight wanes. This is your leafy friend's own circadian rhythm, called "nyctinasty", and it helps the plant to conserve moisture.

Despite its nickname "False shamrock", an *Oxalis triangularis* is not associated with Ireland, it's just that its leaf arrangement resembles a three-leaf clover; it actually originates from Brazil.

Fiddle-Leaf Fig

Ficus lyrata

SUN: Bright, indirect light

WATER: Water once a week, allowing water to drain from the bottom of the pot

FERTILIZER: From spring to autumn, feed with a half-strength, balanced liquid fertilizer once a month

MAINTENANCE: Medium

Warning: *Toxic to animals and children if ingested*

With bold, glassy leaves all the way down its trunk, a young Fiddle-leaf fig is the Instagram-friendly house plant that's suitable for beginners.

Though it's not particularly picky about its environment, some mild maintenance will help it grow. Dust the giant leaves to improve light absorption, lightly prune in late spring/summer, and be vigilant about signs of pest infection, including spots, dark patches or white webbing.

Just watch out: a white sap released from the leaves can be an irritant for skin and is toxic to pets.

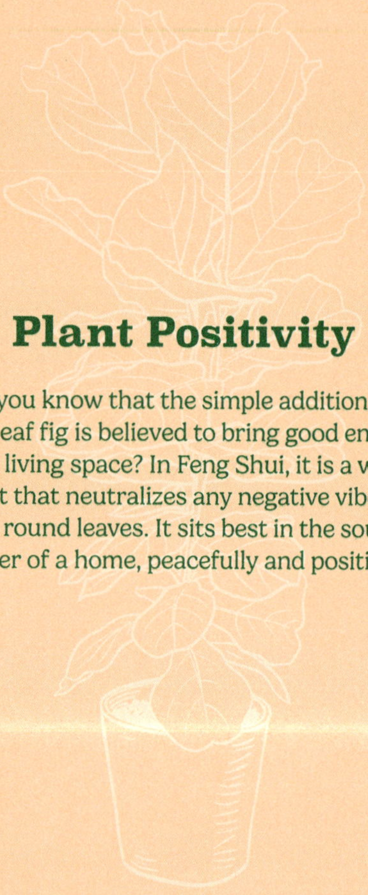

Plant Positivity

Did you know that the simple addition of a Fiddle-leaf fig is believed to bring good energy to your living space? In Feng Shui, it is a wood element that neutralizes any negative vibes with its soft, round leaves. It sits best in the southeast corner of a home, peacefully and positively.

“Flowers are restful to look at. They have neither emotions nor conflicts.”

Sigmund Freud

Flaming Katy

Kalanchoe

SUN: Filtered light

WATER: Infrequently, only when the soil is dry

FERTILIZER: From spring to summer, feed with a half-strength balanced liquid fertilizer every two weeks

MAINTENANCE: Low

Warning: *Toxic to animals and children if ingested*

This cheerful indoor plant will signal the arrival of spring in your home with a bloom of beautiful red or pink flowers that last well into summer.

A Flaming Katy's mood-boosting cycle should continue every year so long as it gets a well-deserved rest at the end of a blooming period. Not many people know that once the flowers have died away, these succulents need 14 hours of total darkness a day, for up to six weeks in order to prepare its blooms again.

Around 10 hours of natural sunlight is just enough to mimic shorter autumn days.

Flamingo Flower

Anthurium scherzerianum

SUN: Bright, filtered sunlight

WATER: Every few days in summer and sparingly in winter

FERTILIZER: Sparingly

MAINTENANCE: Medium

Warning: *Toxic to animals and children if ingested*

The tropical Flamingo flower makes a show-stopper feature for any home. It grows elegant heart-shaped leaves and tall, red leathery flowers that resemble Peace lilies (page 100).

There are a few tricks to keeping them happy, including repotting in spring (usually every other year) to give them space to grow, and try to give them soft water because the roots are sensitive to the chemicals in tap water.

Love your plant and it will love you back: by cleaning the air of harmful pollutants, such as ammonia, leaving your home feeling fresh.

Jade Plant

Crassula ovata

SUN: Keep in bright, indirect light for at least six hours a day

WATER: Water thoroughly when the soil is dry to the touch - always allow the water to drain from the bottom of the pot

FERTILIZER: From spring to autumn, feed with a half-strength balance liquid fertilizer

MAINTENANCE: Low

Warning: *Toxic to animals and children if ingested*

It's not uncommon for a thriving Jade plant to be passed down through families – it's so robust it can sometimes outlive its owners.

The Jade plant gets its name from its fleshy jade-green leaves, but in some Asian cultures the succulent is referred to as a "friendship" or "money plant" and commonly gifted at the start of marriage to signify luck and prosperity.

Thankfully, keeping them healthy is not a huge job, and once a happy Jade plant has settled in your home it can withstand extended periods of neglect. You could say it has a long honeymoon period.

Jasmine

Jasminum polyanthum

SUN: Keep in bright, indirect light for at least six hours a day

WATER: Water one–two times a week, ensuring that the soil is constantly moist but not soggy

FERTILIZER: Feed with a high-potassium liquid feed once a month

MAINTENANCE: Low

Welcome house guests with the natural scent of White jasmine in winter; it smells sweet, musky and floral, as if you've just hung out fresh laundry.

Not only is it beautifully fragrant, the White jasmine plant adds a decorative touch with pink buds and pretty star-shaped white flowers whenever it blooms.

If you'd prefer to keep this sweet-smelling plant in the heart of your home, and not in a more humid space, mist the leaves regularly to give it enough moisture.

Kentia Palm

Howea forsteriana

SUN: Bright, indirect sunlight

WATER: Water once a week, when soil is dry – keep the soil constantly moist

FERTILIZER: From spring to summer, feed once a month with a liquid feed

MAINTENANCE: Low

Introducing the elegant and eye-catching Kentia palm into your surroundings is like bringing a little bit of island life home with you.

It comes from a tiny spot in the middle of the South Pacific called Lord Howe Island – still the only place where these beautiful palms grow naturally.

As such, it prefers certain conditions, such as high humidity, and should be kept some distance from the artificial heat of radiators. Generally, though, it is as easy-going as a typical islander and makes a great choice for beginners.

Palace Plants

During the 19th-century boom in houseplants, the one most-loved by Queen Victoria was the Kentia palm, which she apparently kept in all of her palaces. She even requested that the beloved palms be arranged around her coffin as she lay in state following her death in 1901.

Houseplants Loved by the Royal Family

Fiddle-leaf Fig
Pictured at the California home of Meghan Markle, The Duchess of Sussex.

Parlour Palm
Seen in the living room of Anmer Hall, home of The Prince & Princess of Wales.

Jasmine
King Charles chose sweetly-scented Jasmine to surround his favourite royal residence, Highgrove House.

Boston Fern
Once seen in the background of a video call from Clarence House.

Nerve Plant

Fittonia

SUN: Bright, indirect (or filtered) sunlight

WATER: Water when soil is dry – keep the soil constantly moist and mist leaves frequently

FERTILIZER: Feed with a weak dose of liquid fertilizer once a week

MAINTENANCE: Medium

Another interesting addition to moisture-rich bathrooms is the Nerve plant, originally derived from the tropical rainforests of Peru.

The veins (or nerves) of its foliage can be red or white, which make an attractive accent for often dull shower rooms, particularly when paired with a pretty pot.

If it doesn't like it here, some people display a Nerve plant in a terrarium (page 23), which not helps it to lock in moisture in the plant's environment, but is a charming way to display your new addition.

Orchid

Phalaenopsis

SUN: Bright, indirect sunlight

WATER: Every 5–7 days, using distilled water to keep the compost moist

FERTILIZER: Specialist orchid fertilizer is best after each watering

MAINTENANCE: Low

The ultimate gifting plant, Orchids come in so many different shapes, colours and sizes that you could have a home full of them and rarely receive two that turn out the same.

Some varieties are hard to maintain, which is why the most commonly seen variation is the least demanding "Moth orchid" (*Phalaenopsis*).

These are characterized by long stems and large blooms, often adorned with unusual patterns. Many collectors choose one of the many exotic colours to suit their scheme, while others collect the whole rainbow: from sunshine yellow to sunset coral and neon pink to electric blue.

Painted-Leaf Begonia

Begonia rex

SUN: Bright, indirect light

WATER: Water when the soil is dry to the touch, ensuring the soil constantly moist

FERTILIZER: Feed with a well-balanced liquid fertilizer every two weeks

MAINTENANCE: Medium

Warning: *Toxic to animals and children if ingested*

Forget flowers – fancy leaves are the talking point of a Painted-leaf begonia. Red, purple, green, even silver, heart-shaped foliage with unusual patterns make this an attractive choice for home decoration, particularly as they look good all year round.

Although begonia don't like water on their leaves, they do enjoy a warm, humid environment, so often seem happiest in bathrooms. If the environment is too wet, then light, infrequent mists of water on the leaves should be enough.

Remember to repot them every spring as they grow.

Parlour Palm

Chamaedorea elegans

SUN: Bright, filtered light

WATER: Water when the compost is dry and mist the leaves regularly

FERTILIZER: From spring to autumn, feed with a balanced liquid feed once a month

MAINTENANCE: Low

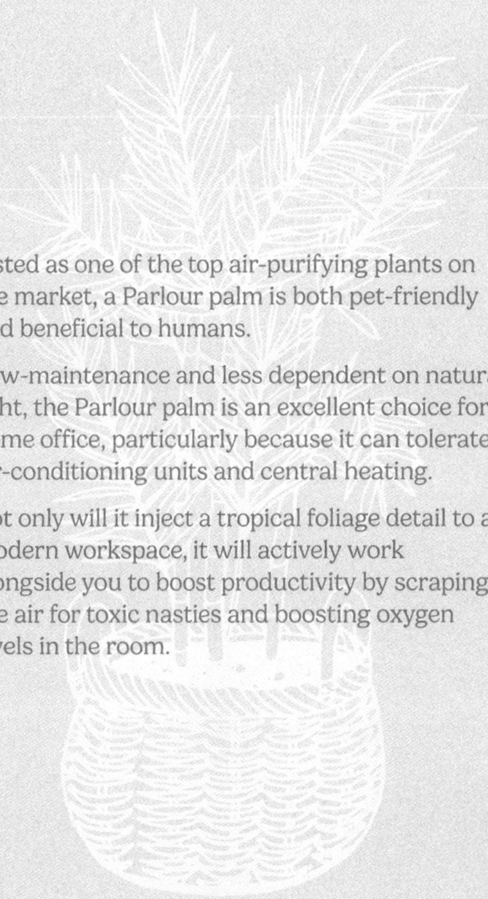

Listed as one of the top air-purifying plants on the market, a Parlour palm is both pet-friendly and beneficial to humans.

Low-maintenance and less dependent on natural light, the Parlour palm is an excellent choice for a home office, particularly because it can tolerate air-conditioning units and central heating.

Not only will it inject a tropical foliage detail to a modern workspace, it will actively work alongside you to boost productivity by scraping the air for toxic nasties and boosting oxygen levels in the room.

Peace Lily

Spathiphyllum

SUN: Can tolerate shade but prefers bright, indirect light

WATER: Water thoroughly when the soil is dry, and mist the leaves regularly

FERTILIZER: Feed with a half-strength balanced fertilizer

MAINTENANCE: Low

Warning: *Toxic to animals and children if ingested*

A Peace lily gets its name from the hooded flowers that look like white flags: a sign of calm and surrender. So, where better to place your plant than a bedroom? The ultimate place of tranquility.

This common indoor houseplant is another one known to improve air quality, which is beneficial for sleep and stress-related headaches. It also enjoys humid environments and releases moisture through transpiration, which can be helpful for allergies and skin conditions.

If nothing else, the attractive lily-like plant is a symbol of calm.

Poinsettia

Euphorbia pulcherrima

SUN: Bright, indirect light

WATER: Water thoroughly when the soil is dry to the touch – always allow the water to drain from the bottom of the pot

FERTILIZER: Feed with a water soluble fertilizer

MAINTENANCE: Medium

Warning: *Toxic to animals and children if ingested*

The perfect pop of festive red and green, a Poinsettia is a popular choice for the Christmas period, often as a household decoration and sometimes a gift.

They like light, draught-free spots in the home and minimal water at the roots: just a regular spritz on the leaves will do. Even with the recommended care, finding the right balance can be challenging, and the plants often die or are disposed of just as the Christmas tree comes down.

Be sure to thoroughly check the plant before purchasing for the best possible chance of keeping them healthy through to the New Year – and even beyond!

Poinsettia: The Christmas Flower

The most popular plant sold at Christmas time even has its own dedicated day in the United States – 12 December has been National Poinsettia Day since 2002 – but not many people know its history. According to Mexican legend, a resplendent Poinsettia bouquet burst from a bundle of weeds one Christmas Eve to symbolize a gift of love to Christ. The more the tale has been told, the stronger its association with Christmas has become.

“Hence, a traveller should be a botanist, for in all views plants form the chief embellishment.”

Charles Darwin,
The Voyage of the Beagle (1839)

Prayer Plant

Maranta leuconeura

SUN: Bright, indirect light

WATER: Water once a week to keep soil moist

FERTILIZER: Feed with a water soluble fertilizer every two weeks, reducing to once a month in summer

MAINTENANCE: Low

Warning: *Toxic to animals and children if ingested*

Each night, a Prayer plant will peacefully bow down its leaves like hands in prayer, opening them back out when it next sees the sun. It's a small yet comforting action that feels like it's saying, "Goodnight".

During the day, this houseplant is quite the showstopper. Its large oval leaves are often two shades of green, intricately patterned with red veins and undersides flourished with fuchsia.

It's not always obvious when a Prayer plant is young and growing vertically, but this is actually a trailing plant that will spread out horizontally, draping itself elegantly off shelves or sideboards.

Purple Heart

Tradescantia pallida

SUN: Bright, indirect light

WATER: Water thoroughly when the soil is dry to the touch, ensuring that it stays moist

FERTILIZER: At the beginning of growing season

MAINTENANCE: Low

Warning: *Toxic to animals and children if ingested*

This striking violet pot plant carries all of the vibrancy of its native country, Mexico.

For a foliage plant, the Purple heart features very little (if any) green shades, instead painting a space almost exclusively in deep purple. And, unlike a False shamrock, it doesn't even flower very regularly.

These qualities make it an easy-to-keep houseplant, which will grow yet more vibrant in the sunnier spots of your home; and, if kept happy, could enrich your decor for many years.

Radiator Plant

Peperomia caperata

SUN: Bright, indirect light

WATER: Water thoroughly when the soil is dry to the touch

FERTILIZER: Feed with a half-strength diluted fertilizer once a month

MAINTENANCE: Low.

The easy-going Radiator plant, as the name suggests, enjoys the dry warmth of an indoor heater. Unlike many indoor plants, they can tolerate extremes of temperature that mimic their tropical South American and Caribbean roots.

They are used to living in the shade of other rainforest trees, so they appreciate indirect light and will therefore thrive in many different areas of the home.

In fact, this plant is so laid-back, it will be happy living under fluorescent lights, making it an ideal choice for an office.

Rubber Plant

Ficus elastica

SUN: Bright, indirect light

WATER: Water when soil is dry to the touch, allowing water to drain from the bottom of the pot

FERTILIZER: Feed once a month with diluted half-strength liquid feed

MAINTENANCE: Low

From the same *Ficus* family as the Fiddle-leaf fig, the Rubber plant was once the most popular of all houseplants, and seemed to be in every household throughout the 1980s.

Thanks to its easy-care nature and potential for impressive room-height growth, it is steadily making a comeback among plant-lovers.

It's known for its beautiful leathery green leaves, which look healthy and lush when properly cared for. Look out for the brooding "Black prince" variety with leaves so intensely inked they look like leather.

Snake Plant

Sansevieria trifasciata

SUN: Moderate, indirect light

WATER: Water thoroughly when soil is dry to the touch, allowing water to drain from the bottom of the pot

FERTILIZER: Feed with a balanced liquid fertilizer once or twice a year

MAINTENANCE: Low

The Snake plant has many nicknames that all point to its razor-sharp leaves: Saint-John's sword, Devil's tongue, even, Mother-in-Law's tongue ...

As they all suggest, this houseplant is made of tough stuff. In fact, it's almost immortal, preferring periods of drought – so don't worry about regular watering – and thriving in light shade.

Often its leaves are beautifully patterned and scaly like a snake's skin, which adds intrigue to home decor.

Folklore of the Snake Plant

The Snake plant is native to West Africa where, throughout history, it was commonly used to shield homes from evil spirits, both practically and spiritually. Not only did the plant serve as a symbolic guardian according to folklore, but its fibrous leaves were strong enough to make bowstrings used in self-protection. This explains another of its nicknames: Bowstring hemp.

"In every walk with nature, one receives far more than he seeks."

John Muir, *My First Summer in the Sierra* (1911)

Spider Plant

Chlorophytum comosum

SUN: Bright, indirect light

WATER: Water thoroughly when soil is dry to the touch, allowing water to drain from the bottom of the pot

FERTILIZER: Feed with an all-purpose liquid fertilizer sparingly

MAINTENANCE: Low

Add interest to your home with a palm-like Spider plant. Hassle-free, interesting to look at and perfect for putting up high when you want to elevate an interior.

The Spider plant is easy to live with, especially if you have pets or little ones. They are non-toxic and even start to improve your living environment from the moment they move in.

A Spider plant will cleanse the air and will also improve moisture levels, which can be beneficial for respiratory issues, skin conditions and sore throats.

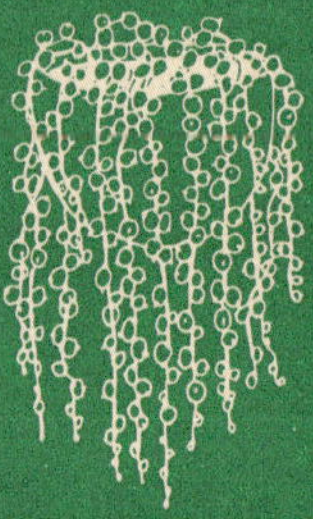

String of Pearls

Senecio rowleyanus

SUN: Bright, indirect light

WATER: Water thoroughly when soil is dry to the touch, allowing water to drain from the bottom of the pot

FERTILIZER: Feed with half-strength water-soluble fertilizer every two weeks in spring and summer and every six weeks in winter

MAINTENANCE: Low

Warning: *Toxic to animals and children if ingested*

These clever succulents store water in their pea-shaped beads, meaning they know how to look after themselves effectively. They look particularly stylish next to vertical plants to create a dynamic display of heights, textures and growing styles.

The vine will grow quickly, gaining between five and 15 inches (13–38 cm) per year and, if you're really lucky, it will produce cinnamon-scented white flowers in springtime.

Swiss Cheese Plant

Monstera deliciosa

SUN: Bright, indirect light

WATER: Water thoroughly when soil is dry to the touch, allowing water to drain from the bottom of the pot, and mist leaves regularly

FERTILIZER: Fertilize once a month with a balanced liquid fertilizer

MAINTENANCE: Low

Warning: *Toxic to animals and children if ingested*

“Monstera” by name, monster by nature.

The climbing plant commonly known as the Swiss cheese plant is easy to keep and fascinating to look at, but it will stretch up and out of its humble home seemingly overnight.

If you can provide somewhere roomie to let this mammoth indoor plant flourish, it will become a superb focal point of the home. And, to help guide it in the right direction, add a mossy pole to the pot and let it naturally wrap itself round it, growing upward like Jack’s beanstalk, instead of reaching further into your room.

Zebra Cactus

Zebra haworthia

SUN: Bright, indirect light

WATER: Water thoroughly when leaves begin to curl inwards, allowing the water to drain fully from the bottom of the pot

FERTILIZER: From spring to autumn, feed with a diluted succulent or cactus fertilizer once a month

MAINTENANCE: Low

More ornamental than a cactus but hardier than an aloe, the miniature succulent known as the Zebra cactus is a curious little character.

They're recognizable for their white-striped tentacles that form as a rosette in small plant pots. They grow extremely slowly and only ever reach a petite 8 inches (20 cm), which means curating a collection of these varied – and undeniably adorable – mini plants could quickly turn into an obsession.

A Zebra cactus also makes an ideal gift because they can be easily propagated from the small offshoots that peel away from the main plant with a little root still attached.

ZZ Plant

Zamioculcas zamiifolia

SUN: Can tolerate low light but prefers bright, indirect light

WATER: Every 2–3 weeks when the soil dries out

FERTILIZER: Feed with a balanced liquid houseplant fertilizer once a month

MAINTENANCE: Low

Warning: *Toxic to animals and children if ingested*

If you're forgetful about plant care, you're safe with a ZZ plant, which is better off underwatered. You could even take off for a short holiday without asking a neighbour to cover your watering schedule.

Many nooks make suitable spots for this tolerant addition, which originates from the dry grassland of Tanzania, sheltered from sunlight by the forest. It will therefore thrive in low light and doesn't even mind a draught.

There is one major drawback: all parts are poisonous, so as well as keeping it out of the way of animals or children, you should wash your hands after contact.

“To plant a garden is to believe in tomorrow.”

Audrey Hepburn